Anna Heart of a Peasant

CAROL MARIE DAVIS

the Peppertree Press
Sarasota, Florida

All rights reserved. Published by *the* Peppertree Press, LLC.
the Peppertree Press and associated logos are trademarks of
the Peppertree Press, LLC.

For information regarding permission,
call 941-922-2662 or contact us at our website:
www.peppertreepublishing.com or write to:
the Peppertree Press, LLC.
Attention: Publisher
1269 First Street, Suite 7
Sarasota, Florida 34236

ISBN: 978-1-936343-83-6

Library of Congress Number: 2011927811

Printed in the U.S.A.

Printed May 2011

To Rachel Anne,
Russell Thane and Amanda Lael

With Love

PART ONE

Beginnings

CHAPTER ONE

In the dead of winter, as fierce winds howled like a pack of wolves across the frozen plains of Byelorussia, my grandmother Anna Kondratevna Anisovich came into the world. The people in the small peasant community of Pristupovschina would recall that night- February 3, 1886, as one of the coldest in memory. Fires in their big clay stoves burned nonstop, and every horse, cow, pig, and chicken was brought indoors to keep from freezing. Even though the moon beckoned brightly, you stayed put- inside- by the fire.

Fortunately, the village midwife, Valeria, who also happened to be Anna's grandmother, lived in the one-room *chata* or peasant house where Anna was born. She had fixed herbal teas and other folk remedies all day to ease the birth for her young daughter-in-law Hanna, who now lay panting on a straw pallet by the fire. With strong, rough hands, Valeria deftly cut the baby's umbilical cord with a distaff (a forked stick used in holding fibers for spinning) the country's age-old symbol of femininity and hard work. If Anna had been a boy, she would have traditionally chopped off his cord with an axe to show in no uncertain terms who would eventually control that household.

Hanna turned her eyes toward Valeria, watching her swaddle her baby tightly in cloth bands from shoulders to toes. She watched and kept silent as the old woman chanted, calling on ancestors to guard Anna from any evil that might be lurking about. For added protection, Valeria attached a good luck charm under Anna's chin then handed her abruptly to Hanna. "Take the child and nurse her for fifteen months or until the next one is born," she commanded. "Yes, *Matuska*," murmured Hanna, a slim, hardworking peasant girl who had been living in the Anisovich household as a recent bride for nearly a year. She knew better than to contradict anything Valeria said, for in the Byelorussian culture of the peasantry, taking orders from *Matuska*, the matriarch, was a perfectly normal way for mothers-in-law to control household members. At the time, Hanna felt relief knowing she had produced a healthy, eight-pound girl, who, in six years would help care for the next children she was duty-bound to bear.

Hanna's husband, Konrad, had missed the whole birth, having downed several glasses of *kvas,* homemade beer, the result of which put him sprawled across the sleeping bench, snoring loudly. Valeria was just as glad her son was out of the way. This was women's work after all.

Valeria wasted little time burning the afterbirth in the stove; if the ground wasn't covered with ice, she would have buried the placenta near the house to appease the *chata's* spirit. The old midwife's pale-blue eyes scanned the place where mother and baby slept quietly and muttered, "Ah, there is one more task to do before I can rest." Taking a deep breath, she threw a heavy shawl over her stooped shoulders, lifted the iron latch on the wooden door and stepped into the frigid night.

The villagers called her "*Babka*" the wise old grand-mother who could predict the future by reading the stars.

She had waited a long time to see what the celestial bodies had in store for her first granddaughter, so she stood fast in the wind and gazed toward the heavens.

The moon in the shadow of Aquarius foretold Anna would live long- she would be clever, strong, independent yet stubborn in her ways. And then, "What's that?" she asked herself, squinting hard. A shooting star seemed to have crossed her line of vision. "Did the planets predict some great misfortune?", she asked herself. The old woman shook her head in disbelief. "How can that be?," she muttered. Reaching for the knotted rag of salt she always carried inside her apron pocket, she untied it and threw a handful of crystals in the wind. "Be gone evil!" she shouted. "You will bring no harm to my little one!" After catching her breath, she went inside and knelt before the Byzantine icon of the Madonna and Child on the wall. Valeria was taking no chances. Besides the ancient rituals she practiced, her belief in Orthodox Christianity was strong, so crossing herself three times, she prayed to the Holy Mother to guard her new grandchild.

For the next three days, Hanna stayed in separate sleeping quarters with baby Anna. According to custom, she was forbidden to do housework, prepare food or even eat meals at the table for fear of contaminating her newborn. Beyond the curtains which divided them, Hanna could hear Valeria banging pots and pans in preparation for the baby's formal introduction to the community. Nothing, of course, had been prepared before Anna's arrival- no blankets, clothes, crib or special foods because it would have brought bad luck. Now everything must be made in a hurry.

Hanna chuckled softly, listening to Valeria shout commands at Konrad. As the male head of the house, Konrad was supposed to give the orders. She knew that her even-tempered husband, who towered over short, stocky Valeria, would do exactly what his mother wanted, though. "Don't worry mama "he said over and over. "We will have everything ready in time." Later, she heard Konrad hammering in the shed as he constructed the crib she, and other Byelorussian mothers favored- a rectangular wooden bed with four sides to be suspended by rope from a ceiling beam. Hanna pictured the crib's gentle, swaying motion calming her child and closed her eyes for some much-needed rest.

When neighbors and relatives showed up at the Anisovich house a few weeks later, they were loaded down with food and gifts. Godparents Eva and Anton brought the ceremonial round rye bread and salt along with the priest from a neighboring town who would conduct the Russian Orthodox baptism. Uncle Jakaw arrived with a soft, fleecy sheepskin blanket for the baby; his wife Pawlina, brought a tiny blouse, embroidered in symbolic red stitches. Jury, their shy ten-year old, offered a little toy horse he wove from straw to give bright-eyed Anna.

"*Dobraha ranku*"(Good morning), boomed Konrad. He was in a lively mood, but stopped short of shaking hands in the doorway because it was bad luck to do so. Instead he greeted friends, neighbors, and relatives inside the *chata*, proudly showing his table laden with refreshments. There were bowls of pickles, stuffed cheese and mushroom *pierogi* (dumplings), warm, nutty-flavored *kasha* (cereal), and sweet honey cakes. By the stove, a wooden spatula in hand, Valeria shouted for everyone to have some *blini*, thick, round pancakes just fried in melted butter.

The new mother traditionally refrained from taking an active role in the ceremony; rather, she stood by the table handing out wooden spoons for the steaming *borscht,* a hearty soup made with beets, cabbage, potatoes and onions. Every now and then Hanna halted what she was doing to glance nervously at Anna who was being paraded around the room. She saw her gurgle and coo as people gushed "Ahh, what a healthy little one," and "Oh, such a pretty baby." Hanna noticed every compliment, and her lips moved ever so slightly after each flattering remark as she muttered the customary oath, "Salt in your eyes," to send the "evil eye" far away from her child.

When the last bit of food was gone, the long-bearded priest began the baptism ceremony, chanting and pouring the holy water over Anna's head. A look of surprise first crossed Anna's baby face and at that point she squirmed against the hands that held her firmly and twisted inside the swaddling clothes that bound her arms and legs closely to her sides. Her chubby cheeks reddened, her little eyes squeezed tightly shut, and then this child that was to become my future grandmother, opened her mouth wide and screamed at the top of her lungs.

During the months that followed, Anna was the center of attention in the Anisovich household. If Hanna was too busy to nurse her, she gave Anna a pacifier of cooked cereal tied in a linen cloth. Mothers in rural Byelorussia introduced their children to solid food as early as the first week of birth in the belief that this would make them grow faster and be able to tackle household chores by the time they reached six or seven years old.

But little Anna knew nothing of work yet. She was showered with affection, hugged, kissed, tickled and sung to. At two years old, she was a sturdy toddler with a thatch of dark hair, sparkling blue eyes, a small upturned nose, and determined chin. She liked to crawl after the chickens under the sleeping loft and pluck flowers from Hanna's kitchen garden. Best of all, she loved to hear Valeria tell stories: of the scary witch Baba Yaga who lived in the forest, and the little Snow Girl whose mother always sang her lullabies before she went to bed. Stubborn as ever, Anna would close her eyes only if Valeria sang the same lullaby: "*Sleep, little Snow Girl, sleep, Our tasty bun so sweet, We'll give you drink a-plenty, We'll give you food galore, And make you such a pretty dress, And teach you four by four.*"

Growing up surrounded by family, Anna absorbed a way of life rich with symbols and rituals. At daybreak she saw Valeria stir the fire in the stove and heard her say, "Thank you, *Domovoi,* for giving us your warmth and protection through the night." The ancestral spirit or *domovoi* resided in the stove and Anna learned to offer it food, especially eggs, so that it would not keep the family awake at night making noises.

When the winter ice melted, the first shoots of wheat poked up in the fields, signaling Spring's arrival in Pristupovschina. Dressed in her new blouse with red sun-shaped circles embroidered on the sleeves and collar to protect her from the "evil eye," Anna was ready to welcome the birds flying back from the south. Hanna gave her little dough-shaped birds to toss in the air and say: "Fly away little birds. Fly to the fields and bring us good luck." Beside her Hanna trilled: "Open your womb Mother Earth and bring out the grass, flowers and plants."

At Easter time, the Anisovich family sometimes attended a candlelit service in the evening at the Russian Orthodox church in the next town. Wherever Anna looked there were lights; glowing and flickering candles shining on people singing hymns of praise. When the altar gates flung open wide, Anna rode on Konrad's shoulders through the smoky haze of incense to the altar for the Father's blessing.

By the time she was six, Anna was a working member of the household sweeping the floor, setting the table, weeding the garden, and baby-sitting her younger sisters Domna, four; Olga, two; and Nadja, just one. She learned quickly to respect the authority of her elders or punishment was swift and harsh; kneeling on dry corn kernels in front of the holy Icon for hours was something even strong-willed Anna wished to avoid. "If you don't teach her when she lies across the width of the sleeping bench, you will not be able to teach her when she stretches out on the whole length of the bench," Valeria warned Hanna.

The Anisoviches, like all the peasants in their community, worked hard from sun up to sun down. Each day Konrad cut firewood, mended tools and cared for their horse Luka while Hanna seemed to do everything else-housework, child care, cooking, feeding the chickens and milking their cow Lina. The cycle of the seasons controlled their lives. In Spring, Konrad harnessed Luka to a wooden plow and cultivated the fields which he later sowed by hand with wheat, rye, barley, and oats. Hanna planted a vegetable garden by the house with beets, turnips, carrots, peas, onions, potatoes, cucumbers, sunflowers, and cabbage, while Valeria cleared an area for the wild herbs she used in healing- mint for stomach aches, nettles for breathing problems, and St. John's Wort, a plant whose yellow flowers cured bruises. She grew garlic to treat colds, sore throats, and ear infections and hung braids of garlic in the livestock shed to protect Luka and Lina from harmful spirits.

In the summer, anyone who could handle a scythe, sickle or rake turned out to harvest the hay in the common meadow. Men did the cutting with their long-handled scythes; the women followed, raking the hay in piles. Entire families, old and young, tied the bundles together and placed them on platforms to keep the hay from spoiling. Midday, the workers picnicked in the fields, enjoying potato *pierogi,* fresh cucumber salad, and crusty brown bread. This was a time for relaxing; children played games and picked raspberries; women sipped hot tea and gossiped about the latest wedding, while the men went off to do manly things like drinking their *kvas* in a shady spot under the trees. Peasant life may have been hard, but it had its simple pleasures too.

Once haymaking was finished, Konrad prepared the field for next spring's harvest while Hanna reaped the cereal crop. Swinging her sickle in calloused hands, she joined the women as they pushed themselves along the rows, singing

Peasant woman at harvest time near a village in Byelorussia by Sergei Mikhailovich Prokudin-Gorskii, 1912. Courstesy; Library of Congress, Prints and Photographs Division, Prokudin-Gorskii Collection

ancient folksongs to *Yaryla*, the goddess of the fields. After the sheaves had dried in the sun, they beat the stems with long-handled sticks to separate the cereal grains from the husks. Sweat rolled down Hanna's neck; clouds of dust swirled and clung to her face. She found it hard to breathe and wiped her face with a kerchief clogged with chaff but continued threshing, for she knew that a good cereal crop would make the difference whether her family had enough to eat, or starved during the long winter.

With the arrival of the summer solstice, the villagers took to the woods to celebrate *Kuppale,* their most beloved holiday. As soon as she was big enough, Anna joined hands with the older girls dancing in circles, singing to *Kupala,* the goddess of the forest. Dazzled by the colorful skirts they wore and the flower garlands in their hair, Anna begged her cousin Safija to show her how to make a wildflower wreath. "Come along with me," said Safija finally, taking her by the hand.

Along the bank of the woodland stream they gathered corn flowers and ferns, wove them into wreaths and tossed them in the water to see which one would float back first. "Whoever has the lucky wreath will be married soon," said Safija. Anna saw hers disappear and sobbed. "Don't worry Anichka," said Safija, wiping her tears. "You will marry when you are old enough. Now, make a wish, because *Kupale* night is a magic time."

Around the birch trees they danced until the leaves took on the sheen of fading light. "At midnight you can hear the trees speak; they even walk from place to place," Safija told Anna knowingly. Anna's eyes grew big with wonder and she wanted to stay up all night to hear the trees talk. As they came upon a clearing in the woods, they saw sparks of

11

light shoot into the sky. The young men had made a huge bonfire and were jumping through the flames in a ritual show of bravery. Anna watched in amazement, rubbing her eyes to stay awake. Afterwards, Konrad found her fast asleep in Safija's lap and carried her home. She would have to wait another year to discover what the trees were saying on *Kuppale* night.

When the first cool autumn nights turned the birch trees a golden yellow, peasants hurried to get things done before the frost. Konrad finished sowing his winter wheat and began harvesting grain, worrying if he would have enough grain for his family and the *kulak* (peasant landlord). The Anisoviches rented their *chata* and surrounding property, paying the *kulak* a percentage of the crops raised on his land in rent. Food shortage was always a cause for worry; in fact, a dreadful famine swept much of the country in 1891 when Anna was just five.

Throughout the last days of fall, Anna dashed barefoot from the fields carrying armloads of dried flax for her mother to comb into long fibers and spin. In addition, she went back and forth fetching water, first to the kitchen crowded with women shredding cabbages for sauerkraut, then to the shed where the men were brewing beer. Only when the grain and root vegetables were stored, the flax processed and firewood hauled from the forest, did the family relax and prepare for the Yuletide season. If a neighbor needed help, like the old widow Tatyana Krasnovich whose husband recently passed away, they would also cut her firewood and patch her roof, for in their small village of less than one-hundred souls, everyone depended on each other to get by, a custom my grandmother would never forget.

At the end of the year, heavy snow blanketed the village.

Wrapped in layers of bulky clothes, Anna looked like some kind of wooly onion with crimson cheeks rolling in the snow. "Papa take me for a ride!" she shouted when she saw her father harness Luka to the family sleigh. Konrad laughed, "Come along, little "*cybula*" (onion), we'll go to the forest to find a spruce tree for the holidays." It was December 24, the start of "*Kaliady*" or Yuletide holidays, a time of merrymaking and following rituals to ensure that the family would have an abundant harvest in the coming year.

They brought the evergreen tree (symbol of eternal life) indoors and its branches filled the one-room *chata* with the fresh scent of the forest. In the cooking area, Hanna baked bread in the shape of a cross and prepared fish for the first ritual meal of the *Kaliady* celebration. Before they began eating, Konrad threw a handful of grain on the table and chanted: "Good health for our people, our animals and our crops."

On New Years Eve, the Anisoviches were invited to a big party at the kulak's house. Showing off their good fortune, Ryhor Besko and his wife Maryna put on a spread for gluttons; there was roast chicken, stuffed fish shimmering in gelatin, a variety of dumplings, sweet fruit desserts, and the main dish of the evening- a fat roasted pig with an apple stuck in its mouth. Entering the room, Anna's eyes opened wide - she had never seen such a display in her life. "Eat as much as you can hold in your bellies," said Ryhor in a generous mood. Later, the guests played party games and went from house to house singing carols, wishing everyone a good harvest and the best of luck in the coming year.

CHAPTER TWO

During the cold winter months, the Anisoviches were forced to spend most of the time in their stuffy, one-room *chata,* a traditional living space no more than fifteen feet wide by twenty-five feet long. In the sub-zero temperatures, their huge clay stove or *pechka,* threw out steady heat, warming Valeria as she sat by its side knitting. The *pechka* took up one-fourth of the room; around it was a busy place where Hanna set the dough to rise, Anna stepped up to stir the soup, and Konrad spread out his tools to carve wooden bowls. The family laundry boiled in huge pots on the stove's wide clay surface, sending swirls of steam through the room. Shirts, skirts, and trousers hung near the chimney drying alongside bunches of mushrooms and garden herbs. Behind the stove, while Nadja napped in her swinging cradle, Olga and Domna played, scattering grain here and there on the straw-littered earth floor for the chickens to peck. At night, the family slept above the stove, or as near to it as they could get, on wooden benches attached to the wall.

With windows shuttered against the cold, the *chata* reeked with the smell of chickens, cabbage, dirty laundry, and wood smoke. Cooped up like this for several months, tempers flared; Anna would shout at Domna, who then teased Olga, who cried and woke up baby Nadja. Hanna, pregnant with a fifth child was exhausted most of the day while Konrad just wanted to escape from all the noise. It was then that Valeria, the *matuska,* took absolute control of matters. "Son," she hollered, "Go feed the animals, chop wood, and visit Jakaw to trade some wooden bowls for a basket of sheep wool!" Knowing he could get his chores done quickly and return home much later after he and his brother completed bargaining over several glasses of *kva*s, Konrad jumped up and was out the door in a flash .

Next Valeria pointed a short, stubby finger at Hanna. "Daughter-in-law, make a soup for supper and see that Nadja is fed and quiet," she commanded. Hanna sighed heavily, picked up Nadja and waddled over to the stove, hoping that was all she must do that day. If she was lucky, *Matuska* would shoo Anna, Domna and Olga to the water barrel by the door, make sure they washed their faces and hands, and tell them to sit at the table in the *krasnyi* or beautiful corner of the room. This was a special place where the holy Icon hung overlooking the family table, and where *Matuska* recounted the ancient stories and folktales they loved to hear.

When Valeria saw the three clean, round faces looking up at her expectantly, she would smile and say, "All right my little "*kurky*" (chickens), now listen quietly." After adjusting her wide figure comfortably on the bench, she began narrating a folktale that has passed down through the generations in my family. It goes something like this:

"Once upon a time, where the forest reaches the sky, live Three Zoryas who tend the dawn, the day and the night. The pechka warms their hut and if you were to visit them, the Three Zoryas would welcome you with steaming tea and hot baked bread. You are always fed and safe from

15

the cold so you would stay the night and sleep next to the warm pechka."

"Grandmother Zorya is first up with the dawn. No matter how much pain she feels in her hands, she rekindles the pechka and slowly shuffles out of the hut to the corral of the Sun Horses. She calls them softly and they come neighing, waiting patiently as her old fingers unlatch the gate. Sometimes her hands are so frozen from the cold it takes longer, but she never fails to swing open the gate. Then, with a burst of energy, the beautiful white horses snort and break into the sky, releasing the light of the sun in glorious gold, pink and orange colors.

The Maiden Zorya is next to rise, always making her way from the hut into the day. On a clear afternoon you might see her move across the blue sky, sending her strength to open the blossoms on the cherry tree or gild the fields of wheat. If she disappears, perhaps she is only gathering mushrooms deep in the sky forest, but always she returns back to the hut, spent and ready for supper.

When the light begins to fade, Mother Zorya, the Keeper of the Night, walks to the gate of the corral where the Sun Horses trot to greet her. She waters and feeds them and shuts tight the gate as the shadows deepen, melting into the dark. But there is one more task to do before her daily work is through. She must feed the dog chained to the stake in the sky. And so she brings some meat scraps to the hungry animal. He is thin and shivers, but gobbles up all the food. "Don't worry, I never forget you," she says to him. The dog of destruction is satisfied then. He lays down and Mother Zorya makes sure he is chained securely to the pole star in the Little Bear constellation before returning back to her warm hut in the forest."

When she finished, the children clapped their hands and cried for more. "That's enough for tonight," she said lighting the oil lamp on the table. The pungent smell of cabbage filled the room and then a blast of cold air broke through as Konrad entered. He took his place at the head of the table and Hanna immediately served the hot soup and bread. "Will the bad dog in the sky ever get loose and gobble us up?," asked Anna, before dipping her spoon in the communal soup bowl. "No, never, my little "*cybula*," said Konrad laughing, for he had heard this story many times. "Now, eat your soup."

Spring arrived once more like a breath of fresh air in Pristupovschina. Cherry trees blossomed alongside the weathered log buildings; new greenery sprouted in the fields, and the Anisovich family welcomed Ivan, the first boy in their family. Since his birth coincided with Easter, he was carried to the church in his new linen swaddling clothes along with Hanna's *Pasca* (traditional Easter bread) to be blessed at the altar amid clouds of incense. For the celebration, Anna dyed hard-boiled eggs red, (the life color) with onion skins, and helped make the christening *kasha*. Valeria, as usual, prepared stacks of round *blini,* the ancient symbol of new life even as she began to feel the pangs of old-age herself. In a year, the ritual would be repeated again for Vassily, their sixth child.

As the eldest girl, Anna found herself taking on more household responsibilities while her parents worked in the fields. During the next few months, still burdened with the care of her younger siblings, she also helped the old grandmother whose knees and hips were stiffening with age. Cautiously, she left Domna, now six, in charge of the younger children, while she tended Valeria, bringing her hot tea and soup. "You will be the one I tell my secrets to," she told Anna pulling her aside one day. Anna, listened solemn-faced as her grandmother revealed how she planted crops by the phases of the moon. "When the moon is new, it pulls water up from the earth so put the cabbage seeds in at that time," she began. Anna nodded as Valeria continued: "Sow beans and peas in the second quarter, when moonlight is strong because they will make healthy seeds inside the pods. Only after the full moon, when energy goes into the roots, can you plant the beets, carrots, onions and potatoes," she warned.

On sunny days, Valeria showed Anna how to strip peppermint leaves and set them to dry in a shady spot. "A hot cup of peppermint tea will cure chills, fever and upset stomach," she advised. When the chamomile plant growing by the doorstep bloomed, she picked the flowers and instructed her granddaughter how to make tea for troublesome monthly periods, and how to make a poultice for skin inflammation. By late August, garlic, the Russian penicillin, was harvested and Valeria showed her how to mash the pungent cloves with a little oil and wrap them in wool to cure an ear ache or chest cold.

Day after day, when she was able to get up and hobble to the stove where she liked to sit, Valeria passed on her knowledge to Anna. "You will become a midwife, a healer," she told her one bright sunny morning. Anna felt a lump of pride and fear rise in her throat at the same time; pride that her grandmother singled her out, and dread for that awesome responsibility. She shuddered, "Why me, Grandma?" she asked. "Because you are the oldest; you saw how your baby brothers came into the world, heard the chants, know the rituals, now listen and you will learn more," she said and proceeded to tell Anna what teas and other herbal remedies to use, the special incantations to say, and other information needed to deliver a healthy baby. Later she would impart her knowledge of the stars; to interpret how the constellations were aligned at the date, time and location of someone's birth, predicting their destiny.

One day, as the shadows of the afternoon lengthened, Valeria asked Anna to make a cup of raspberry tea to ease her aching joints. "I can not teach you anything more now," she said sipping her tea slowly. Perched on a stool, Anna leaned closer to hear her grandmother's fading voice. "Whatever bad luck that comes into your life, you must not be afraid of it," she whispered. A long sigh escaped her lips and then she added: "Anichka, it is important for you to know that you are powerful, beyond what you can imagine." Anna, a bit puzzled, nodded and said, "I will remember, Grandma," but she wondered what her grandmother meant and why she stopped revealing secrets. Perhaps she's tired, she thought. "I will let you rest now," she said, tucking the shawl closer around the old woman's shoulders. Seeing Valeria close her eyes, Anna tip-toed off to peel the potatoes for supper.

When Konrad and Hanna came in from the fields, the children ran to greet them. "How is *Matuska* feeling today? asked Hanna as she washed her hands at the water barrel. Quickly, she glanced at the figure sleeping by the fire and called out at once, "Husband, see to your mother, now!" Konrad dropped the water ladle and ran to Valeria's side. He lifted his mother gently in his arms and kissed her pale, withered cheek. Then he looked up at Hanna and the children and said quietly, "Mama has passed away."

They dressed Valeria in her best white linen blouse emblazoned with red symbols of the sun and placed her tenderly on a bench in the Icon corner where she faced the image of the Blessed Mother. Her folded hands held a lighted candle; by her side was her spindle, a loaf of bread and a lump of salt. The priest administered the Orthodox last rites and, weeping, the family carried the coffin to the cemetery where Valeria was buried just before sunset, so the solar disc could light the way to her future life in the vast dark beyond.

With Valeria gone, Anna felt a sense of loneliness in the crowded *chata*. During the long, dark winter months, she moped about as she swept the floor, thinking of the times she sat by Valeria's side listening to her stories, smelling the fresh mint leaves in the garden or studying the stars at night. "It is time you learned some useful, skills," Hanna remarked one day, thrusting a distaff in Anna's left hand. Now that Valeria was not there to boss her around, Hanna was fast becoming the *matuska* in the Anisovich house.

The holy icon of the Virgin of Vladimir, a 12th Century painting, artist unknown. Anna prayed to a similar icon of the Blessed Mother many times. Original in the State Tretyakov Gallery, Moscow

"Take some of the fibers between your finger and right hand thumb and twist them together," she ordered. When the thread was drawn down and became long enough, Hanna tied it to the top of a spindle (a top-like rod with a disk-shaped weight attached to the bottom), and gave it a turn. Anna saw how the weight pulled the fibers through her fingers, while the rotation twisted them together into thread. "That looks easy," she thought, but by the end of the day, all her efforts showed only sore fingers and a batch of tangled, uneven threads.

"Well, that won't do," said Hanna the next day as she prepared the loom for weaving and told Anna to stay nearby and watch. After she warped the loom, Hanna pumped the two foot pedals to lift the alternate pairs of warp threads for her shuttle to pass through. "Clack, clack!" it sounded after every throw of the shuttle released her finely woven weft threads in an even line. At first Anna saw only white linen cloth appear, then Hanna switched to a shuttle wound with red thread and intricately wove a pattern of crosses and four-sided figures in a wide band of red color. "This is our language, our tradition," explained Hanna. "We weave our souls into this cloth to remind us of our ancestors and the invisible threads that tie us all to *Dziady* (God)."

Because most peasants in Byelorussia were illiterate, woven cloth or *ruchnik* was used as a sort of textbook or visual aid for understanding the world around them. The length of cloth, whether an arm-span, person's height, or length of the wall in one's house, was a way of structuring space; of attaching a human dimension to it. The white linen center symbolized the Outer World where the ancestors resided; the woven red bands at the beginning and end of the cloth represented a time dimension between the living and the dead. Infused with such power, the cloth was believed to protect the wearer from harm.

"Is this cloth magic?" asked Anna pointing to a newly woven *ruchnik* on her mother's loom. "Yes," she answered simply. "When you marry, this will tie you and your husband together and bring good luck to your new life." Hanna, like all her forbearers, thought the *ruchnik* acted as a talisman, bringing happiness and prosperity to those who believed in its magic properties.

Most of the weaving, however, was used for everyday needs. Straight pieces of white linen cloth were sewn into shirts, dresses, tablecloths and covers for sleeping. When it came to embroidering geometrical ornaments on sleeve tops and cuffs, necklines and hems, Anna was impatient. Her short, broad fingers produced wide, crooked stitches in the cloth until Hanna would throw up her hands in despair. "Anna, you're good only for field work," she would say, pulling the cloth away to redo herself.

Released from this tedious work, Anna pictured herself digging in the rich black earth, planting onions and marigolds, mint and cabbages as soon as the weather warmed up. She thought how she would bring her straw mattress to the threshing shed in the spring and sleep there at night, breathing in the fresh smell of hay instead of the stuffy, smelly air of the closed-in *chata*. The threshing shed functioned as an extra sleeping area as well as storage for grain. Other unpainted log buildings such as the livestock shed, wood shed, and the family's outhouse stood in the back overlooking the fields.

The peasants in Pristupovchina were once serfs of the landed gentry and the wealthy owners of vast fields. Although serfdom was abolished by Tsar Alexander II in his Manifesto of Emancipation of 1861, my grandmother's family, and others really had no place to go when freed; they were bound by their agricultural way of life and their cultural traditions, so they stayed in the fertile southern-steppe province where their ancestors had lived for generations. A few crafty peasants, like Ryhor Besko, managed to buy some of the less fertile holdings from the nobility and they became *kulaks* or peasant landlords, but they still had to pay high taxes on the land and the surrounding buildings.

In that closely knit community where ritual dictated how they must live in order to survive, Anna felt a sense of security knowing that her life would follow the cycle of the seasons; she would work the land, marry, have children and eventually be put to rest in the place where she was born.

CHAPTER THREE

By the time she turned sixteen, my grandmother Anna's world suddenly seemed more exciting. She had grown into a beautiful young woman with a full-blown figure and long dark hair that reached down to her waist. Although only four feet eleven inches tall, she made up for the height she lacked with a vibrant personality. When the village boys began calling her to join them in the meadow, Anna just laughed at them, showing off her even white teeth and rosy lips that turned up at each corner. "Go home to your mothers," she taunted them, hands on hips. "You won't ever find men as strong as we are!" they would shout again. Picking up her skirt, she flounced off barefoot across the fields without even a backward glance at the boys whose hopes she had crushed like the broken sheaves from last season's harvest.

Anna had her sights set on eighteen year old Sergei Michailovich, who lived in the village at the end of their narrow unpaved street. She admired his broad shoulders, flaxen hair and intensely blue eyes. When he left for work each morning with his horse and plow, she would bound across the rows of broken top-soil to flutter her kerchief at him. Sergei would halt the horse, wave back and seem to blush, but always he continued with his work. Day after day, Anna wished he would do more than just stop and waggle his hand at her. Perhaps this summer at the Kuppale feast, she thought, they would hold hands and dance together in the meadow.

Before this time, however, Anna got her wish. "Anna, beautiful Anna, come walk with me, I have something to tell you," she heard Sergei say one warm spring night. She was walking toward the threshing shed when he caught up with her and took her by the hand. Surprised, she let her fingers tighten around his and looked into his eyes. "What is it you want to say?," she asked breathlessly. "Oh, Anichka, I have wanted to be with you for so long, but was too shy to tell you, and now I think it is too late," he whispered. Before she could question why, he bent his face close to hers and kissed her. When the kiss was over, he gazed at her with a burning look. "I have been drafted in the Tsar's army and will be gone tomorrow. Will you wait for me?," he asked, holding her tightly.

Anna's head was spinning. Her first kiss and now the love of her life was telling her he would be gone for who knew how long? "Yes, Sergei Michailovich, I will wait," she found herself saying. He opened her hand and placed a small round stone there and said, "So you won't forget me."

The next morning the whole village turned out to mourn him. The peasants knew Sergei might never return home because life in the military was harsh- ferocious discipline often included beating soldier recruits with fists, scabbards, or whatever was handy. Scanty rations and over-crowded, bitterly cold barracks were other conditions they would have to endure. Despite all that, the peasant soldiers were famous for their bravery, loyalty and hardiness. It was said that in war, the Tsar's soldiers stood their ground until they prevailed over the enemy, were wiped out, or were ordered by their superiors to retreat.

Along the roadway, after being blessed by his parents, Sergei began marching eastward toward Great Russia. As he passed the familiar fields he stopped and turned his head for one last sight and saw Anna waving goodbye, the stone he had given her pressed closely to her lips.

CHAPTER FOUR

"Anna!" screamed Olga waving her hands frantically as she dashed across the wet fields in the early morning fog. Anna stopped tilling the soil and looked up, surprised to see her sister running towards her. Gasping for breath, Olga blurted: "The baby is coming, hurry!" Anna dropped the hoe and put a hand up to her mouth. Her mother was just eight month's pregnant, it was too early for the child to be born now. "Run, find Aunt Eva, while I see to mama," Anna said, turning quickly in the direction of the *chata*. When she entered, there was Hanna crumpled on the sleeping bench by the stove, breathing heavily. "Help me child!" she groaned. "There is no time to waste!"

The color drained from Anna's face. Even though Valeria had instructed her in the art of midwifery years ago, she felt terrified at what she must do now. With shaking hands, Anna stoked the fire and put a pot of water to boil. Sweat trickled down her face as she examined her mother, trying hard to recall the things Valeria had taught her. Instantly, she saw the baby's head crowning, and with another groan, her mother pushed out the tiniest baby Anna had ever seen. It was a boy. Anna caught the infant and placed him in her mother's arms. She knew Valeria had traditionally severed her brothers' cords with an axe, but there was little time to look for one in her father's shed. Instead, she found a kitchen knife to cut it, tied it securely, then washed the infant and wrapped him in a blanket.

Hanna, white-faced, was still moaning by the fire. "Put the baby in the crib; I can not nurse him now," she said panting. Anna did as she was told, then fixed her mother a cup of herbal tea. "Drink this mama, it will make the pain less," she said quietly. When the placenta was expelled, Anna and her mother both breathed a huge sigh of relief just as Olga and Eva came rushing up. "A new boy has arrived, go in and see him," Anna announced, pleased that she had handled the whole birth without her aunt's assistance.

On a bright June morning a month later, Anna looked out the doorway at the sun-soaked fields and wished she could be out there with the family. Everyone had left to pick the late spring peas; everyone except the new baby Piatro and Anna. Because she was menstruating, Anna was considered "unclean" and it was taboo for her to touch any plants. So reluctantly, she closed the door and began her chores.

Piatro was a happy baby, content to lie in his swinging cradle near the stove as Anna boiled potatoes and buck-wheat kasha to bring to her family for their mid-day meal in the fields. She sang a lullaby as she changed his diaper and placed him back in the cradle. He was sleeping when she swept the straw on the dirt floor and put it in the stove to burn. When it was time to carry the food to the workers, Anna hesitated a moment, then decided not to wake the baby.

Walking back to the *chata* with the empty dinner pails, Anna lingered to admire the lilies growing by the stream. She bent down to breathe in their fragrance, and then stood up and smelled a whiff of smoke in the air. As she neared the *chata* she saw a grey plume rising from the thatched roof and her heart started pounding. Dropping the pails in the grass, she raced to the house crying. But she was too late to save her baby brother; Piatro lay motionless in his cradle in the smoke-filled room.

When there was a death in the family, certain rituals took place. Piatro was given the Orthodox last rites, placed head first under the Icon in the sacred corner, and then carried to the cemetery to be buried before sunset. Immediately after, purification to rid the *chata* of the evil spirit that may have caused his death was carried out. It was swept clean, all water discarded, and my grandmother Anna, whom they felt responsible for the tragedy, was sent away.

PART TWO
Changes

CHAPTER FIVE

"Anna Anisovich, you will never learn a thing!" screamed the kulak's wife Maryna. Grabbing the fish from Anna's hands, Maryna slapped her across the face with it. "Stupid girl, you must always gut a herring from head to tail!" she shrieked. "Now get out of here! You belong in the stables!" Anna wiped her smarting cheek with the tip of her apron and stalked off to the livestock shed without a word. Ever since she had been sent away by her family to the Besko's farm, she had worked as a slave in Maryna's kitchen beaten often for not scrubbing the floor clean enough, or for cutting the cabbage too thin. Better to be with cows and horses than around the nasty kulak's wife, fumed Anna, shaking her head in disgust.

Awake before dawn with only a chunk of hard bread for breakfast and no tea, Anna began her new chores milking the cows, chopping ice from their water troughs, pitching manure in a pile by the shed. By noon she was working in the fields until the sun went down. A bowl of cold, watery soup and a piece of dry bread awaited when she dragged herself back to the barn. Climbing into the hay loft, she gazed at the stars through the cracks in the rough log walls, the barn cats nudging against her as she thought of Sergei, hoping he was still alive. Resentfully, she pictured her family sitting around the table eating hot bread and soup, and fell asleep heavy-hearted.

Out of the corner of her eye, Anna would often notice the kulak's younger son Pawluc lurking around the shed or staring at her between the branches of a tree. With his piggish eyes and pock-marked face, she thought him ugly and shouted at him many times to go away. Usually her harsh words were enough to make him stumble off on his short bowed legs, muttering the whole while.

One day though, emboldened by the vodka he snuck from his father's hiding place, Pawluc approached Anna with a gaze so fierce it made her skin crawl. He ignored her shouts to leave and pounced suddenly, grabbing her by the waist. Of course, Anna would have none of that. Thrusting her knee hard into his groin, she pushed him away with all her strength. Doubling over, Pawluc fell backward into the manure pile, groaning. To make sure he got the message that his advances were unwelcome, she picked up the manure fork and told him boldly that she would use it if he ever grabbed her again.

When word of Anna's deed got around the farm, the peasants made fun of Pawluc. "That just shows he's not a man," they laughed, poking each other. But Maryna didn't think what Anna did to her son was funny. Storming out of the kitchen, she caught Anna by the hair and dragged her into the yard to beat her with a stick. Anna's broad Slavic face reddened, her blue eyes blazed as she twisted free, seized the stick, broke it, and threw it on the ground. Furious, she fled over the fields into the forest. "And don't come back, wicked girl!" she heard Maryna yell after her.

But return, Anna did. It was after nightfall when she crept back into the stable to get her things. She was looking for her shoes and blanket when she heard a voice in the darkness. "I had a feeling you would return," whispered Tadevus, the old peasant who took care of the kulak's horses. Anna stood still. "Don't be afraid," he said, "you will need these for your trip." Anna peered into the shadows and saw the old man holding out a sack. "Take these potatoes and cabbage from the mistress' garden, along with my bread and salt, and be on your way quietly." Anna reached for the sack and said, "Thank you grandfather, you are very kind." Quickly she added her other things and slung the bag over her shoulder. "May the *Domovoi* protect you from evil, child," said Tadevus as Anna hurried into the uncertain night. My grandmother was seventeen.

CHAPTER SIX

She kept to the bank of a stream walking miles until daylight touched the trees. Ravens cawed to each other in the branches; the acrid smell of wood smoke hung in the air. In a moment she caught sight of brightly painted caravans and small campfires burning in the distance. "*Cyhani!*" (Gypsies) she whispered under her breath. Barely did that word leave her mouth when a pair of snarling dogs charged up the bank toward her, lips curled back over bared fangs, fur on their hackles raised.

"Dziki!, Brudny!, Stop!," shouted a tall, dark-skinned man sprinting up behind the animals. They stood still now, whimpering, tails between their scraggy legs. "What brings you here, peasant girl?" asked the Gypsy, studying Anna's disheveled appearance; the frayed blouse, dusty skirt, worn shoes and the bulky sack she held. Anna twisted the sack nervously, then straightened her back. "I've left home to seek my fortune," she answered, gazing directly into his dark eyes. "Well, well," he said. "If you want to know your fortune, you've come to the right place, but it will cost what you have in the bag."

Anna slung the bag over to him. "My name is Janos, come with me" he said, catching it and gesturing to a campsite. Anna followed his swinging stride down the embankment where a young woman in a full, brightly-colored skirt sat tending a fire next to an ornately carved wagon. "This is my wife Tsanka, she will make you welcome," he said tossing the bag near the fire. Anna introduced herself and showed the potatoes, cabbage, bread and salt she had brought. "It's not much, but it will make a good soup," she said, forcing a smile. Tsanka gazed up at her through heavy-lidded eyes. The gold bracelets tinkled on her wrists as she reached for Anna's hand. "Give me your palm," she said.

Anna expected Tsanka to tell her fortune by studying her open palm, instead she searched her face. "You are running from evil," she began and spat over her left shoulder. "There is a long road ahead of you, but I see honesty in your eyes. You can rest here," she said, releasing Anna's hand and pointing to her covered wagon. Suddenly Anna felt very tired. Yawning, she entered the caravan, crawled next to the three dark-haired children who lay sprawled on rumpled blankets, and closed her eyes.

Darkness had settled in when Anna awoke to the stirring sounds of violins and laughter. Women in billowing skirts, their eyes reflecting firelight, danced barefoot, leaping and whirling like a bevy of colorful butterflies. She saw a group of singers stamping their feet and clacking wooden spoons to the rhythmic melodies. Half-naked children ran shrieking around the campfire, their dogs chasing them and barking. She smelled meat sizzling on the fire and heard Janos shout: "Come out, peasant girl. Come join the wedding celebration."

Pulled into a circle of dancers, Anna felt the freedom of the music; now quick and playful like children romping, then fast and furious like a troop of soldiers rushing into battle. When the fiddlers stopped, Tsanka grabbed hold of her. "You dance well for a "Gadje" (non-Gypsy) she said. "Tonight we feast; tomorrow you will become one of us."

In the months that followed, Anna wandered with the Gypsies through small hamlets and villages as they played music for weddings, mended pots and pans, and told fortunes. Tsanka took her into the secrecy of her painted caravan and told her Gypsy folktales, sang their songs and taught her how to tell fortunes. Anna learned how to read tarot cards and tea leaves. "Swirl the tea with the left hand three times in a cup, but never a white cup," said Tsanka. "White is for mourning. Turn the cup upside down to drain and right side up again," she instructed. "If you see a bird, that's good news. Clouds mean trouble. A flag is danger," and so she went on.

Adopting the solemn, mysterious tones of a Gypsy fortune teller, Anna joined Tsanka whenever they came into a new village. With her fair skin, slanted blue eyes, and gold coins enhancing her dark braided hair, Anna looked exotic and peasants flocked to have their fortunes told by her. Ever watchful, Janos collected their money and quickly moved the caravan on to another village.

After three years of roaming the countryside, camping in farmer's pastures and in remote valleys, my grandmother felt tired of Gypsy life. She wanted to settle down on a farm, to feel the rich black soil and see vast fields of wheat turn golden in the sun. One day when they were camped near a village where two brooks joined a river, she looked at the neat wooden houses along the roadway, the horses and cows grazing in the grassy meadow, and the endless rows of crops growing in the fields. That night she said goodbye to Janos and Tsanka.

An elderly woman in a kerchief and spotless white apron answered the door of a small farmhouse when Anna knocked. Years of hard work and suffering had twisted her body, yet she had a kind face and smiled at the girl standing before her. "Do you want something to eat?" she asked, for strangers often came begging at her doorstep and she never turned them away without giving them a bowl of kasha or a piece of bread. Anna shook her head. "I need to work," she answered, extending her hands so the woman could see the calluses on her palms.

"My name is Ruth," the woman said inviting Anna into a clean front room that held a table and some chairs against a wall. She told her how difficult it was to manage the small farm since her husband died. "My daughters have married and moved away, and my only son does not want to be a farmer," she said, her voice quivering. Touched by the old woman's tale, Anna reached out and patted Ruth's gnarled hand. They agreed that Anna would help with housework, prepare meals, as well as tend the garden and join the seasonal workers cultivating the soil and harvesting wheat, rye and other grain crops. For this she would receive wages, food, and a warm place to sleep.

Whenever Ruth's son Alaksandar came home from his studies, Anna listened in awe to the stories he told of the widespread poverty in the little villages he encountered and how Tsar Nicholas II was responsible for the backward and oppressive conditions of the peasants. "The Tsar imprisons the people," he declared hitting the supper table with his fist one evening. At first Anna could not believe the things he was saying. After all, didn't her family and every peasant family she knew put the Tsar's picture next to the holy Icon in their *chata* as a sign of their respect and loyalty?

Alaksandar persisted, voicing his views with each visit. "The royal family eats pheasant, asparagus and ice cream while the common people go hungry," he stated showing a picture of the Romanovs dressed in all their finery at an elegant banquet. Anna had no idea what ice cream or asparagus were but she thought the Tsar's family was entitled to eat whatever they wanted. "I think the Grand Duchess Anastasia looks beautiful," she said, trying to change the subject. "Wake up Anna! The Russian Empire has become the fifth largest industrial power on earth through the sweat of workers who are paid next to nothing," Alaksandar declared, his face turning crimson.

Alaksandar sensed things were changing and was making plans. Even before Berlin declared war on Russia, he and his mother had fled the farm, leaving Anna alone to determine her future destiny. She was twenty-eight years old.

CHAPTER SEVEN

A nna had always shooed away the men dressed in dark suits who visited Ruth's farm advertising good paying jobs for peasants in far away places like America. After Ruth and her son left though, she decided to listen closely when an agent from the Russian-American Steamship Line stopped by as she was packing. He showed her a photograph of the SS Czar, a magnificent new ocean liner, and said for fifty rubles, the price of a ticket, she could sail away to a brighter future. "You can make piles of money working for rich, kind Americans," he told her.

The agent had only to look at my grandmother's strong arms and knew just where she would be needed: wealthy American housewives were clamoring for domestic servants in New York. Spitting on his pencil, he scribbled some words on paper and said that he would arrange all transportation to Hastings-on-Hudson, a small river town in Westchester County, New York. There, he assured her, a better life was waiting for her.

Anna acted immediately. She took the agents' papers, paid her fare from the wages she had earned and caught a ride in a farmer's wagon that evening. Along the country road, a full moon illuminated sleepy villages with fields of newly planted wheat as far as the eye could see. At intervals, the wagon driver halted the horse and people came out of the shadows to climb aboard. It seemed that many, like Anna, were leaving the hardships they knew in hopes of finding a better life somewhere else.

At first light, Anna woke to the scene of rolling green hills. Gradually, high-storied brick buildings and golden onion-shaped cathedral domes rose up above the hilltops and then, there she was, in Minsk, the capitol city of Byelorussia. At the grandly embellished Byzantine-style train station, she stood staring at a huge locomotive chuffing down the tracks billowing clouds of black smoke and coal dust; its wheels screeching to a halt at a platform mobbed with people. Sellers of tea and spices, wine and sausages, tickets and newspapers, hawked their wares. She saw dozens of peasant families waiting, some of them sleeping on stacks of baggage, and finally she joined them to await the iron monster that would carry her to the Baltic Seaport city of Libau and then across the North Atlantic to America.

A burly stationmaster showed her where to board, and gripping her bundle in one hand, ticket in the other, she climbed into a third class carriage and found a seat among other hot and musty-smelling travelers. When the train picked up speed, leaving the sellers and the city behind, did she fear what lay ahead? Would she miss those she left at home? If she had any such anxieties, she kept them hidden; there was no time to think about such things. She had made a decision and she was going to stick to it, no matter what.

From her grimy window she saw Minsk fade in the distance replaced by thatched houses and farm buildings on the open plains. Women in kerchiefs and men in straw hats stopped planting to stare as the train whistled past their fields. Crossing the vast Belarusian forests thick with oak, pine and birch, startled roe deer and giant hares scampered into the trees. It thundered though ancient river valleys, around the lakes and grasslands of Lithuania, stopping periodically to fill its water tank and coal box, to haul freight and pick up passengers. When a cloud of iridescent blue and ebony butterflies soared past her window, Anna saw them as a good luck sign and thanked *Dziady* for blessing her journey. At the next stop she bought bread from a vendor by the tracks and scattered some crumbs for the woodland spirits.

Back on the train, Anna offered bread to her fellow passengers, for it was the custom to be hospitable, even to strangers on a train. A middle-aged woman, clad in a flowered kerchief, patched skirt and apron spoke to Anna in Trasianka, the Byelorussian dialect familiar in Anna's village. She recounted the harsh conditions in the factory where she had worked; the humiliating treatment by the bosses, the fourteen-hour working days, the widely ignored safety regulations and the dirty crowded barracks in which she lived. "Now, I'm going to America where the streets are paved with gold!" she said patting the pocket in her skirt where she kept her ticket hidden. Anna smiled and said how she, too was traveling there. She and the older woman were among the tens of thousands of Eastern Europeans emigrating to the United States at that time.

After a six-hundred mile journey on the train, my grandmother arrived at Libau, the main emigration port on the Baltic Sea. There she was met by a representative from the steamship line and taken to a quarantine building where she and other immigrants were observed for disease or medical problems. Through an interpreter, Anna was asked questions which she answered as the agent had instructed. What is your name? "Anna Anisovich. "What is your age?" "Twenty eight." To the question, "What is your occupation?" she replied, "I am a housekeeper." The inspector wrote down "Domestic" on her form. When asked "Are you insane, an anarchist or a prostitute?" she became indignant and scowled. "Of course not!" she said loudly. The man glanced at her fierce blue eyes, then quickly stamped some official-looking forms and thrust them in her hands. She had passed her first test in becoming an *Amerykanski*. Suddenly Valeria's final words flashed before her: "You are powerful beyond what you can ever imagine," she had told Anna. "Stay with me Grandmother," Anna whispered softly. "I know there will be more hardships along the way."

The following week, clutching her new passport, Anna waited among the passengers bound for America. Before them the ocean liner SS Czar lay in port: a massive boat, larger than any cathedral and soon to be filled with more than a thousand people. Immigrants trudged up the gang-way and into the ship, holding fast to their children and all

The Steamship Czar, the ship that carried Anna and Vincenty both to America, although they traveled separately- Vincenty in 1912 and Anna in 1914.

their worldly possessions. Most descended into the bowels of the ship, towards the steerage section where they would live in damp, close quarters for two weeks or more.

Below deck, Anna stepped cautiously on the metal stairs still wet with disinfectant from cleaning up the stench of the last boatload of passengers. As her eyes adjusted to the dim passageway, she followed the slim woman walking ahead. "The males stay on one side, females on the other," said the young woman pointing to the bunks separating the small space. Her self-assured manner indicated she knew how to maneuver around the ship and for Anna, who could neither read or write, this was a blessing. "I am Lea," said the woman smiling. Anna introduced herself. "As you can see I am just a poor peasant but I am going to America," she said holding her head high." "Well, I am going there also, to be a seamstress in New York," said Lea extending her hand. In less than an hour they were sharing experiences and navigating the ship, arm in arm.

At dinner time, they sat on the edge of their bunks, balancing their meal of bread, porridge and potatoes on metal plates in their laps; there was no dining area for steerage passengers. When darkness came, they pulled the curtain that divided the men from the women, shook out their own feather quilts (the ship did not provide bedding), lay down on their narrow bunks and closed their eyes. They listened to men snoring, babies crying and the constant pounding of the ship's engines until Anna could stand it no longer and got up to walk on deck. Exploring the ship with Lea, they followed the sound of accordion music and discovered a dozen or more people singing by the main deck amid barrels and coils of rope. Men and women clasped each other against the lurching of the waves and sang familiar songs of their homeland. Some were happy tunes, others so mournful that Anna felt she would cry. "Oh why did I ever leave my country?" she asked herself silently.

Near the end of the voyage, Anna looked out to sea on a grey, cloudy day and noticed that the horizon seemed to rise and fall as the ship rolled to the wind. Suddenly she heard a shout- "All passengers down below, a storm's coming!" She ran down two flights of metal stairs, then two more, and another two until she reached the steerage section. Once everyone was inside, the doors were slammed shut and locked to keep anyone from falling overboard. In the darkened space without air fit to breathe, people soon panicked and became seasick. Children cried in terror; a woman screamed hysterically: "The ship's going down, the ship's going down!" Anna clutched the bunk rail to keep from falling as the ship pitched violently throughout the night.

Fortunately, the next day dawned bright and clear. Anna once again stood on deck breathing the fresh ocean air, relieved all had survived the storm. Without warning the ship's horn blasted sending passengers scrambling above to see what was happening. Then, there it was in the distance, the Statue of Liberty, America! Anna's hand fluttered up to her face, her eyes became misty; she had made it to this new land, now what? Crossing herself three times, she prayed that she made the right decision while all around her, people cheered. It was July 29, 1914.

For the next several hours, Anna and Lea waited with the steerage passengers for the ferry to take them to Ellis Island. With name tags pinned on their shawls, they followed the crowd of immigrants into the Great Hall. All day long, through an intricate series of metal-railed passageways, they filed in long procession, step by step, bearing bundles and trunks and boxes. In the confusion the two new best friends became separated, never to see each other again. As Anna inched her way to the Medical Inspection Station, she watched a man have his eyelids pulled inside out to check for the dreaded eye disease Trachoma. When it was her turn she felt some pain but it was over quickly as was the rest of the physical exam. It seemed the doctors at Ellis Island were adept at briefly scanning immigrants for obvious physical ailments just by glancing at them. Anna, who was always hale and hearty, was pronounced fit, with no contagious diseases that would endanger the public health. "So far, so good," she sighed, working her way to the final inspector, the one who would decide if she would be allowed to stay in America or be deported. Through an interpreter the questions began: "What is your name and where do you come from?" "Do you have money to take you to your final destination?" "Are you joining a relative or friend?" Do you have a job waiting?"

Anna took a deep breath and answered the first questions easily. When asked if she had fifty dollars or less, her hand nervously patted the sewn pocket in her skirt where a few crumpled rubles (Byelorussian currency) lay concealed and nodded. Next came the trick questions: "Are you joining a friend or relative at your final destination and do you have a job waiting?" Looking directly in his eyes, she repeated the lie that the steamship agent told her to tell. "My brother will meet me in Hastings-on-Hudson, New York and help me find work." The agent had told her that if she informed the inspector that she had a job already lined up, she would be in trouble and sent back to her old homeland. The sly agent knew that there was a law in the United States that said immigrants couldn't be promised employment that might take jobs away from those already living in America.

The inspector glanced at her papers again, stamped them and reeled off a list of instructions: "Get your foreign money exchanged here, take the railroad ferry to New York City and board the train to your destination." Bewildered, Anna looked about the huge room with its mass of foreign signs and people speaking different languages and did not know where to go or what to do next. Suddenly, she felt a tap on her shoulder, and the interpreter, an official-looking woman with a kind face said, "Let me help you."

Anna's Journey From Minsk to America

PART THREE
Adapting

CHAPTER EIGHT

My grandmother arrived at the quaint railroad station on the late evening train from New York. No one came to meet her, so she found a bench by the tracks and sat down to wait watching the sun turn a brilliant orange before it set behind the palisades along the Hudson River. She heard factory whistles blowing, freight trains chugging by and thought what a busy place this village of Hastings was. The stations' electrified lamps turned on, illuminating the deserted platform and still she waited. When the ticket clerk locked up the station for the night, she continued sitting on the bench, a dark solitary figure with a bundle at her feet.

The clerk saw the name tag still pinned to Anna's shawl and muttered to himself, "another foreigner who doesn't know her way around!" Advancing towards her, he growled, "You can't stay here. Go to the 'foreign section' where you belong," and gestured with his thumb to the row of rundown tenement buildings along the waterfront. Anna did not understand what he was saying so she stayed put, glaring at his face. He turned on his heel and walked off in a huff, up the hill to the local police station and came back with a young constable. "Come with me miss," said the policeman in a friendlier tone, "I'll take you to your people."

55

He brought her to a boardinghouse overlooking the tracks and left when a stout woman in a dirty apron opened the door, a kerosene lamp held out before her. "So another one comes knocking. Well, come in, you can pay your rent at the end of the week," she said in a Slavic language that Anna understood. Her name was Irina and she managed the three-storied tenement building without heat or running water. "Follow me," she said breathing heavily as she climbed the rickety stairs to a narrow landing on the top floor. "The room is in the back," she told her, descending the steps with the lamp, leaving Anna to feel her way along the wall in the blackness. A young girl, no more than fourteen stumbled to the door, rubbing her eyes when Anna tapped. A cracked window let in the streetlamp's glare illuminating three women stretched out on mattresses on the bare floor. "Find a spot, they will pick you up in the morning for work," muttered the girl in a Polish accent.

My grandmother's introduction to America was typical of many poor immigrants; they settled in ethnic neighborhoods where they shared the same customs, language and foods. After working a twelve-hour day as a domestic servant for a local family with five children, Anna actually looked forward to socializing with the Russian, Ukrainian, Hungarian, and Polish immigrants in her building. Irina offered the boarders simple, comforting meals such as *haluski* (Ukrainian stuffed noodles), *Kapusta* (Polish sauerkraut), Hungarian red peppers, and Russian borscht.

On warm nights, the front porch became a meeting place where they gathered to sing, drink, play cards and get to know each other better. Anna liked to tell fortunes saying, "you will be lucky in love," or "someone will give you money soon." She knew what people wanted to hear and rarely disappointed. One evening a tall, good-looking young man by the name of Vincenty Casmirovich Ovchook walked up to the group with a pitcher of beer. Anna had often admired his lean, muscular shape as he crossed the footbridge at Washington Avenue on his way home from work. Now he smiled at her and she accepted the beer he offered. "Give me your palm handsome man; I will tell your fortune," she said, looking deeply into his trusting brown eyes, her mouth curling up at the corners.

She told him there had been danger in his past. He replied, "Yes, I served in the Russian army and saw many terrible things." She kept her eyes fixed steadily on his and said, "You will be successful in your work." A look of interest crossed his face. "I work hard. Why shouldn't I? I want a better life for myself and the family I want to have someday." Anna squeezed his strong hand, bent her head closer and murmured, "You will have a long life, Vincenty Casmirovich, and many children." He swallowed his beer, not taking his other hand away from hers. "Ahh, you're good," he whispered, bewitched by her gaze.

They talked into the night. Vincenty told her he had arrived in Hastings two years earlier lured by the promise of work on the railroads and in the factories. When he revealed he was from Korduny, a small farming village in Byelorussia close by her own place of birth and that he had crossed the Atlantic on the SS Czar, the same steamship as Anna, her eyebrows raised in astonishment. Did you know my family in Pristupovschina? she asked hopefully. He replied that he never met them. "I'm sure you miss them as much as I miss my parents," he said showing her a letter from his brother that he carried folded in a worn leather wallet. "Can you read and write? she asked, surprised once more. He shook his head and explained that the priest in Korduny had written the letter and the local priest in Hastings had read it to him. "I would like the priest to write to my family if I had some good news to tell them," said Anna sighing. Vincenty searched her eyes for a long time. "If you will be my wife, would that be good news?" he asked quietly. Anna dropped

Anna & Vincenty Olchick pose for their wedding photograph. They were married at Saint Stanislaus Kostka Church in Hastings on Hudson on September 15, 1917. Photographer unknown.

her gaze and nodded. They were married by that same local priest two years later at Saint Stanislaus Kostka Church in Hastings on September 15, 1917.

After they were married, my grandparents Anna and Vincenty Ovchook, or Annie and Vincent Olchick as they were called by the local residents, moved into a two-room apartment on the south side of the ravine near the railroad tracks. Vincenty earned less than two dollars a day as an unskilled laborer but with Anna's additional housekeeping salary, they were able to afford the larger place and even buy a bed, table and some chairs. When the babies started arriving though, five in five years, Anna was forced to stay home and things became more difficult. Vincenty took on whatever extra jobs he could find: handyman, day laborer, scavenger of coal and wood scraps. Anna planted a small garden in the ravine and for a while the family had turnips, cabbage and carrots in their soup. During the great 1918-1919 Spanish influenza epidemic, they were so busy trying to make ends meet, they had no time to dwell on how sick they were from the virus that killed thousands. Anna's garlic infused soups and rubs pulled all of them through that awful time.

Anna finally made contact with her family in Pristupovschina and learned through her sister Nadja that they wished her well. Events in Russia were changing fast: Tsar Nicolas II, his wife Alexandra and all their children were murdered by the Bolshevik secret police. A new communist society was being formed that was supposed to raise the standard of living for the people. Instead, as far as Nadja was concerned, it was more difficult to earn a living or buy food. "Dear sister," wrote Nadja, "It is a very hard time for me. We have nothing to eat because my children are little and I am unable to work. Please do not take offense that I have to ask you for help. Would you send me anything?" Anna then would reach into the tin box where she kept their meager savings and visit the priest at Saint Stanislaus to have a letter written, enclosing a few dollars for Nadja; two more for the Father.

On July 10, 1926, after years of scrimping and saving every penny, Anna and Vincenty realized the American

The Olchick house at 4 Spring Street, Hastings on Hudson viewed in 1929 at the end of their quaint lane. Photo courtesy of the Hastings Historical Society

dream- they bought a home of their own. With a $600 down-payment and a mortgage of $1,928.90 from the Hastings-on-Hudson Co-Operative Savings and Loan Association, they became the proud owners of a house and property at 4 Spring Street, Hastings on Hudson, New York.

Their new home, located a short distance from the center of the business district looked like it had weathered many years of sun, rain, wind and snow. A pair of unpainted wooden additions attached to the main structure were small and box-like, dating back to who knew when. A wagon shed, two-seater privy and a couple of small lean-tos where rodents and feral cats lived long before the Olchicks ever took over, also spoke of a bygone age. The house lacked electricity and centralized heating, but to Anna, the place was grand. It had cold running water, a wood stove and plenty of rooms- nine of them plus an attic and two stone cellars. "Just right for a growing family," thought Anna happily when she first saw the place. In the back of her mind though, she had plans to rent the extra rooms to immigrants and pay off the mortgage as soon as possible.

On moving day, Anna and Vincenty loaded their possessions in a wagon and hand-pulled it along Railroad Avenue, up hilly Valley Street and into the small lane off Spring Street. The five Olchick children- Sophie, eight; Antoinette, seven; Carl, six; Peter, five; and Joseph, four, raced ahead, eager to see their new home. "Wait for mama and papa," called Sophie, running to catch up with the three in front as she clutched her littlest brother Joseph's hand. Sophie (my future mother) took her responsibilities seriously and often looked worried; as if the weight of the world was balanced on her thin shoulders; quite the opposite of her younger sister Antoinette who was carefree and lively and would rather run off and play with her brothers than stay at home.

On the porch beneath the low-pitched roof, the Olchick children stared uncertainly at the jutting corners of the old house, the long stone-paved yard, the weathered sheds and the odd-shaped windows that seemed to wink at them in the hot summer sun. All five squealed when a small creature sped past their feet and disappeared under the wagon shed door. "That mouse will soon be some cat's dinner," laughed Vincenty wiping the sweat from his brow as he began unloading the wagon, looking for the bread and salt that must be brought into a new house before anything else. "It's here, Vincenty," called Anna removing the package she carried in her large apron pocket. She placed it on the black cast iron stove and motioned for her family to enter their new home.

CHAPTER NINE

Although a member of St. Stanislaus Church, my grandmother carried a multitude of long held pagan superstitions into her new home. "Never greet someone with a kiss or shake hands across the threshold. Never go back into the house once you left because this would bring bad luck," she warned. Whistling indoors attracted the devil and it was a bad omen if a bird landed on the windowsill or a black cat crossed her path. Fearing her life would "break up" if she tore a piece of bread off with her hands, she always cut it with a knife, holding the dark rye loaf against her apron and slicing away from her body. Compliments should be avoided, likewise talking about one's success. "If someone says something flattering you must always mutter 'Salt in your eyes!'" she cautioned.

Anna could hardly wait to begin tilling the rich black soil in the small garden area, planning for vegetables and herbs here, grape vines and sunflowers there, apple and peach trees by the fence. She bought a few chickens and rabbits, envisioning the tasty stews she would prepare and when the children begged for a dog, a mixed-breed named Buddy joined the family. Anna looked around her, at the children playing in the fenced-in yard, the garden sprouting greenery, at her new house filled with family and the promise of renters living within, and she felt truly blessed. "Thank you Dziady," she said, wishing the people back in Pristupovschina could see how well her life had turned out.

In many ways Anna remained a peasant at heart. Untouched by the American culture she moved halfway across the world to enter, she made jam and red wine from the plump concord grapes that twined up a trellis in the back, canned green beans, tomatoes, pickles and sauerkraut from her kitchen garden, braided the stems of garlic and onions and hung them above the stove, along with mint, chamomile, rosemary and thyme to use for cooking and healing. She relied on folk medicine to treat any illness, from crushed garlic for cold symptoms to plain old spit to ease a bug bite. "Put a sliced potato on your forehead and the pain will go away," she would tell Vincenty when he complained of a headache. Another not-so-traditional cure came directly from the ancient Russian steppes where Cossacks used the rich black soil to staunch their battle wounds. Anna also believed ancient incantations were necessary in healing and sadly remembered the time her little brother died because she forgot to say the chants that could have avoided the "evil eye".

Once confined to a crowded tenement apartment, Sophie, Antoinette, Carl, Peter and Joseph now felt the freedom of running barefoot exploring every nook and cranny in the old house. To them the place was mysterious: there was the little closet under the stairway where Carl would hide in the dark, listening for his brothers and sisters foot-steps when playing hide-and-seek; the attic with its uneven creaking floor and dusty old trunks beckoning to be opened. Going under the porch to the cellar for Anna's homemade sauerkraut or a pail of coal was an adventure only Sophie,

*Anna & Vincenty in front yard at 4 Spring Street a few years
after they purchased their house and property. Ca 1934*

the eldest, was allowed to do. She would creep down the
stone steps holding a flickering candle in one hand, feeling
her way cautiously along the damp earth floor to the shelves
stacked against ancient stone walls. If something moved, she
would screech and run back upstairs, afraid of the rats that
lived in the darkness. "Go back and get what I asked for,"
Anna would insist, for she would not accept her daughter's
fear as a reason for disobeying orders.

When the school authorities came around, Anna was suspicious at first but she recognized the opportunity for her children to receive an education, and besides, it was the law. All were enrolled in the local Hastings school and later joined a new recreation program geared toward assimilating them into American ways. The Olchick kids were bi-lingual, speaking English in school and Trasianka, a Byelorussian dialect of the peasantry at home because Anna stubbornly refused to give up her native tongue.

In her new home, there was no doubt that Anna was the "matuska"- the matriarch in the family. Short of stature but strong of arm and will, everyone did what she ordered; it was easier that way. If Anna called the children for supper, Sophie rounded up her brothers and sister to the table quickly before a wooden spoon smacked their behinds for being late. Even Vincenty kept his visits short with friends in the Municipal Park because if Anna wanted him home chopping wood, she was known to charge across Valley Road with blue eyes blazing like two hurricane lamps toward the bench where he and his cronies sat schmoozing and scream: "Get home, you peasant!" Vincenty knew better than to argue or the rolling pin she clutched behind her long skirt would come out next, swinging in her broad fist.

CHAPTER TEN

My grandfather Vincenty left childcare and household matters up to Anna. That was women's work after all. He took on the traditional men's role of worker and chief provider for the family. Before he landed a full-time job for the New York Central Railroad Company, one of the largest American railroads operating in the Northeast, he hauled freight along the waterfront and did odd jobs for the wealthy folks in town. If there was a fence to mend, roof to patch, or trash to haul, he was the man for the job. Come the weekend, though, he was down by the river catching shad, eels and crabs, returning home when he felt like it or when his pail was full with fresh fish.

When it came to renting out rooms in their house, the whole family pitched in. Vincenty, gregarious and talkative, recruited immigrants from work while Anna baked extra loaves of dark rye bread and always had a large pot of soup ready for the hungry Portuguese, Polish, Hungarian and Russian lodgers returning from work. The children grudgingly cleaned up afterwards, except on Friday nights when they were shooed off to bed early. Friday was payday for the lodgers who liked to spend some of their wages drinking and gambling in their rooms and Vincenty made sure the renters had a good time by offering Anna's homebrewed red wine, ignoring Prohibition laws which made it illegal to manufacture or sell alcohol at the time.

In the summer of 1929, Vincenty started working on the railroad, teaming up with a gang of men who welded and spiked down steel rails, replaced heavy wooden cross ties, and cleaned the ballast underneath when clogged with mud, snow or ice. Strong and sinewy from years of physical labor, he lifted the thirty-nine foot jointed rails as easily as the younger laborers, although he had to wear a truss everyday to relieve the bulging hernia on his side.

The Olchicks felt life was good in Hastings until the 1930's ushered in the years of the Great Depression. Although Vincenty was employed full time on the railroad, his friends were not so lucky. It was a time when one out of every four Americans was out of work. The lodgers he had recruited soon lost their jobs, fell behind in their payments and began roaming the country in search of work. Vincenty's salary failed to meet the rising costs of warm clothing and heating coal. Subsequently the children became sick with upper respiratory infections, sore throats, chills and high fevers which Anna's folk medicine could not cure completely. All five developed diphtheria and only four children recovered. Eleven year old Joseph died of this dreaded childhood disease and Anna was devastated. She and Vincenty spent all their savings to give him a proper Russian Orthodox funeral and laid him to rest in Saint Joseph's Cemetery.

Throughout the Thirties, trouble seemed to lurk behind every doorway in the old house on Spring Street. Wind whistled through holes in the ceiling where plaster had crumbled from long exposure to rain and snow. It seemed whenever Vincenty climbed his rickety ladder to patch one hole in the roof, another appeared the next day. Dark rooms

(Top) Sophie Olchick and Antoinette Olichick (bottom) pose in tattered coats for unknown photographer on Spring Street, Hastings. Ca 1930

took on the smell of mold and mildew. To make matters worse, Anna's supply of preserved food was dwindling, turning sour in the dampened cellar. The children roamed the streets in tattered coats looking like the urchins Hastings resident Lewis W. Hine captured in his photographs of poverty-stricken Americans.

Whenever he had a chance, Vincenty supplemented the family meals by using his fishing skills to catch sturgeon, shad, and eels down by the river. There were many fish in the unpolluted Hudson at that time. Peter and Carl tagged along setting traps for crabs, exploring the waterfront, looking for old rags, pieces of rope, metal- anything they could pick up and sell for a few pennies to the local junkman. When bored with this, there was an old weather-beaten shipwreck along the shore that they were forbidden to climb on, but they did anyway, pretending to be sword wielding buccaneers.

Carl Olchick sits in front of Hastings High School. Ca 1934

It was one of those swashbuckling adventures that ended in tragedy when fourteen year old Peter fell on a rusty piling that ripped through his leg. He did not tell anyone for days about his accident until it was too late. The wound festered, tetanus infection spread throughout his body and a week later he died of lockjaw. Filled with grief, the Olchicks laid their second son Peter to rest next to Joseph on a rainy autumn day in October, 1935. To help pay the funeral expenses, Sophie and Antoinette left high school and went to work as maids for local residents.

Carl was next to drop out of school, but for a different reason. He missed his brothers; the camaraderie they shared laughing at each others' jokes, playing ball in the park and even using their fists when taunted by schoolyard bullies. Always a sensitive child, he brooded, withdrew to his room, pulled down the shades, and took solace in playing long mournful notes on his violin. Anna, sick at heart, catered to Carl, her last remaining son. She allowed him to stay home, offered his favorite meals, placed good luck charms on his clothing and prayed to the Blessed Mother to keep him safe.

Seventeen-year-old Sophie and sixteen-year-old Antoinette grieved over their brother's deaths but looked outward. They saw how well the families they worked for lived. They touched the stylish dresses the ladies wore, tried

Sophie, 17 and Antoinette Olchick, 16, in their new rayon dresses. Ca 1935

on their high-heels, smelled their perfume, and they wanted to have the same nice things. Like rebellious adolescents, they kept part of their salary and bought skirts that swayed round their slender hips, rayon dresses that outlined their rounded bosoms and waistline curves. They had their hair permed in soft, flattering waves, rouged their cheeks to make their faces glow and sprayed Evening in Paris on their wrists.

Pretty soon young men in town began to notice the attractive Olchick sisters. When Antoinette dated and became pregnant, the young fellow she went with refused to marry her so she decided to give the baby up for adoption. But Anna would have none of that. "The child will grow up strong within this house!" she stated, arms crossed firmly across her chest. Some months later, with Anna as midwife, a healthy baby girl named Sylvia was born in the back room of her kitchen three days before the Spring Solstice. Still hoping to get married, Antoinette again became pregnant and her older sister Sophie helped Anna cut the umbilical cord on a sweet-faced baby girl named Rosita, born at home on a sunny day in May. Anna vowed to keep this child also, for in her ancient beliefs she viewed life sacred; children meant the continuation of the family and Anna's own immortality.

Antoinette did marry, but moved away, leaving Rosita and Sylvia for her parents to bring up. Anna, now in her fifties, enlisted Sophie's support, and just as she had looked after her brothers and sister when they were youngsters, Sophie changed baby diapers, sewed little red gingham dresses for her nieces as they grew older, and tied pretty ribbons in their hair. Carl, pleased at becoming an uncle, helped out when he could, watching the children play in the yard when Anna was busy indoors and Sophie at work.

When the girls became school-age, Anna marched over to Saint Matthew's School, with Sophie as her interpreter, to convince the Franciscan sisters that Rosie and Sylvia needed a Catholic education. "The Blessed Mother must watch over them since their own mother is not here to do so," said Anna, who figured divine intervention and the nun's strict teaching methods would benefit her granddaughters as well as ease her own child-rearing burden. The nuns agreed and offered scholarships to both children.

PART FOUR
Memories

CHAPTER ELEVEN

Sophie wrote the date she met my father in her diary- it was April 4, 1936. She was barely eighteen years old when Paschal "Patsy" Venuto rolled into Hastings in a friend's Model T and swept her off her feet. Whenever she could escape from Anna's control, she and Patsy danced to the music of Benny Goodman's Orchestra deftly copying Ginger Rogers and Fred Astaire's fancy foxtrot steps from movies like "Shall We Dance" and "Swing Time." For a fifteen-cent theater ticket, they could leave the hardships of the Depression Era behind and enter the happier, fantasy world of Judy Garland in "The Wizard of Oz." Screwball comedies like "Bringing up Baby" with Katherine Hepburn and the comedic antics of Charlie Chaplin made them laugh and forget that they had little money and a war was brewing on the horizon.

Five years after they met, Sophie and Patsy were married in a simple ceremony. There was no time for a grander wedding celebration because the Second World War had started and Patsy was sent overseas to defend America. I was born nine months later. On a cold February night, Anna looked up at the stars and foretold a life of hard work, marriage and many children in my future. No matter that she predicted this for each and every one of her children and

Sophie Olchick poses at the Ardsley Country Club in 1937

Pasty Venuto sits on fender of car while visiting Sophie Olchick before they go dancing. Photo Ca. 1937

grandchildren; it was the message she wanted all of us to understand- "You must work hard and be fruitful!"

With the nation at war, meat, butter, sugar, canned food and even shoes, always in short supply in the Olchick residence, were now impossible to obtain due to military needs. Anna worked overtime in her garden and kitchen, putting up jar after jar of preserved cucumbers, tomatoes, beans, and sauerkraut. In the village, Civil Defense air sirens issued their mechanical screams unexpectedly, warning everyone to run, take cover, and prepare for a possible enemy attack. My mother told me that her heart would skip a beat whenever she heard those sirens or saw the light blue-and-white Civil Defense logo on emergency vehicles in the neighborhood.

Throughout the war, people in Hastings showed their patriotism helping families like mine whose loved ones were serving abroad. My mother received baby clothes and blankets, tins of Carnation milk and even a baby carriage from well-intentioned folks in town. This pleased Anna, for

My grandmother Anna holds me for my first photograph to send overseas to my father Pasty Venuto who was serving overseas during World War II. Photographed by my mother Sophie in April 1942

she remembered how people in Pristupovschina helped one another. "Help the weakest and always hope that for you, too, there will be help when you need it," she said quoting an old Russian proverb. When my father returned home from the war, he was warmly received and offered a job as a groundkeeper in nearby Hartsdale.

My mother named me Carol after Carole Lombard, her favorite movie star, but I was always Carolka to my grandmother. "Carolka, stop bothering the cats!" she'd yell or "Carolka, stay out of my garden!" It was Carolka this and Carolka that in her Byelorussian language that I could understand but never speak myself. Growing up under my grandmother's roof, I often felt she was a tyrant. When my sister Priscilla, was born Anna used a primitive type of babysitter to watch her while my mother Sophie was at work. Priscilla was harnessed in the middle of a sturdy, seat-less chair with low, unmovable legs that prevented her from moving about the floor. This way, Anna kept an eye on her while she cooked supper. I had to sit at the kitchen table quietly and watch as she pounded round loaves of bread, or tossed vegetable peels out the back window into a compost heaped with coffee grinds, egg shells and other organic waste. Sometimes, she told us folktales about the witch Baba Yaga who lived in the forest in a chicken-leg house and ate children, but if she was in a good mood, she'd bring out her tambourine and thump it while singing old gypsy melodies.

When I was young, the house seemed full of mystery; I could hear things at night when I was supposed to be asleep. There was a hole in the floor above the kitchen where my cousins and I looked down and spied on Anna drinking tea and telling fortunes. "Watch out for strangers,"…"Beware the evil eye,"…"Someone will give you money," she'd tell the ladies coming to visit. We were careful to listen for the sound of footsteps on the stairs, or smell a whiff of pipe tobacco meaning that Grandpa was coming to see that we were all tucked in bed.

Summer was my favorite time of the year. I remember the old-fashioned pink roses that climbed the picket fence, smell their sweet fragrance and smile when I think how I tried to make perfume by mashing their petals in a jar of water. The four of us-Sylvia, Rosie, Prissy, and myself went barefoot all summer, stamping in puddles, climbing over the garden gate, running through the earthy rows of mint and radishes. Indoors, we played in the attic jumping on the lumpy mattresses left over from the days the lodgers slept there and sometimes we snuck into the damp and musty cellar looking for buried treasure. Those old stone walls surely held secrets we thought, poking into the crevices with

The four of us- left to right; that's me, age 7, next to my cousins Sylvia, age 12, Rosita, age 10, and my sister Priscilla, age 3 posed in front of Grandfather Vincenty's wagon shed. My mother photographed us on Easter 1948

our sticks. "I bet runaway slaves could have hid here a long time ago," said Sylvia, who had a vivid imagination and had recently studied the history of slavery in school. She knew that the Underground Railroad was an escape route to freedom and that many fugitives went north via the Hudson River. Our imaginations knew no bounds in those days as we pictured people running for their lives under the cover of darkness, and finally coming to our house for safety.

Our front porch was a gathering place for evening songs and great drama. My cousins and I staged musical comedies dressing up as Ginger Rogers in hand-me-down gowns, tripping over the long hems while singing "Hoop-Dee-Do" at the top of our lungs. If it rained, so much the better. We set up a chair for Anna to watch our rendition of "Singing in the Rain" and other favorite songs from "South Pacific." Mary Martin had nothing on us as we piped "I'm goanna wash that man right out of my hair," while actually washing our tresses with Sylvia's prized Halo Shampoo in the pouring rain.

I can recall one particular rainy day that could have turned into a tragedy. Anna warned us to stay on the porch that day, even though it was just showering lightly and no lightning flickered above. She must have felt something in the air, for no sooner had she issued the warning, then the huge sumac tree that had hung over the side of our house ever since I could remember, cracked in two and crashed down right in front of us.

When Antoinette visited with her other children, Dorothy, George, Joey, Eileen and Johnnie, we squeezed around Grandma's table and munched brown bread sprinkled with sugar and drank tea with mint and lemon. In the evening we laughed fluttering our hands in front of a kerosene lamp, making birds and animals jump around the

My grandmother Anna's kitchen photographed by an inspector for the village of Hastings on Hudson in 1956. Notice the number 1 placed on the window to identify this room for the eminent domain process that was to claim the Olchick house and property. Photo courtesy of the Village of Hastings on Hudson, New York

kitchen's old plaster walls.

My grandmother features strongly in my memories. She forbid me to bother the wild cats that hid under stacks of old wood in the darkest corner of the wagon shed. "Cats catch rats, so leave them alone!" Anna would shout emphatically. The females had dozens of cute, furry kittens, so irresistible I risked bites and scratches from their fiercely protective mothers just to find and pet them. When neighbors complained that there were too many, Grandpa set a trap for a particularly fertile female and had my father take her to Hartsdale to set loose in the woods. Two weeks later she was back, a little skinny and dirty, but none the worse for wear. "The heck with what people say, this cat stays here," stated Anna, putting out a saucer of milk and crumpled bread by the shed. Looking back, I think my grandmother identified with that poor creature who, against the odds, returned to the only family she knew. For Anna, family meant everything, and she continued setting out milk each day for the cat I later named Spunky. Spunky continued providing kittens for years to come.

If I wanted to find Anna in the house, or avoid her for that matter, I had only to look in the kitchen where she spent most of her time. Up before sunrise, she would have the fire in her wood and coal-fired stove rekindled, ashes scattered on the compost, the bread dough swelling and coffee boiling before anyone else was up. I recall how the stove made the small room stifling hot in summer even with the windows open, but there was my grandmother, ignoring the heat, wiping her brow with a towel or apron, cutting onions and potatoes for the soup of the day.

On Sunday mornings she whipped up *blini,* thick round pancakes smothered in butter and sticky honey and served straight out of the pan. At Easter time, she showed the four of us how to color hardboiled eggs with beets and onion skins, and we waited eagerly for her *Paska* bread to come out of the oven fragrant with the aroma of yeast. Grandma's round oak table was seldom without a flowered tablecloth and forever cluttered with potted plants, jars of tea, sugar, flour and cereal boxes that we had to push aside to make room for dinner plates, but there was a coziness about it that I miss today. Whoever came visiting was welcomed with hot tea, (served in a jelly glass), and a chunk of warm brown bread- an old custom she never failed to observe.

If Anna was not in the kitchen, chances are you would find her in the garden, sleeves rolled up, bent over her plants telling them to grow strong and be fruitful. Before it ever became popular in Hastings to put potato peels, fish tails and other organic waste into the ground as fertilizer, my grandmother was using these scraps to make her vegetables and flowers vibrant. Giant marigolds and daisies blossomed between rows of parsley and beans. Cabbages were huge, tomatoes fat and juicy, and even the garlic grew in such abundance that she had enough to last the whole year- all grown without the use of pesticides or store-bought fertilizer.

Garlic was an important ingredient in my grandmother's medicine bag, used for practically any ailment. Ear ache? Out came the crushed garlic wrapped in cotton and stuck inside our ear. Sore throat? Garlic mixed with ugh, hot milk and butter was the cure. We reeked of garlic in school, for we had to go to classes regardless of runny noses or stomach aches. If any of our classmates complained, the nuns gave them stern looks although that did little to ease our unpopularity.

CHAPTER TWELVE

I remember the letters my grandmother received from her sister Nadja in Byelorussia: "I am writing to you, my dear sister because I want to know if you are safe and sound …" "I have two children, Zina and Lyubov…", "Our father is deceased now, we buried him near mother…" With the fear of communism quickly spreading in America, those little scraps of paper filled with fancy Cyrillic script stopped coming during the 1950's and Anna felt their loss deeply, for she had no close relative to share her sorrow when her last surviving son Carl died from pneumonia in 1954. I could see the worry lines etched on her face and hear her deep sighs as she knelt in front of the Icon praying.

One day, near the end of February, 1956, when it was so mild that the winter snow on the rooftop was practically gone, I came home from school to see my mother and Anna talking to a man on the front porch. I saw the man give an official-looking letter to Anna and thought news from Nadja had finally arrived. When I saw my mother's jaw drop as she read the letter, I hurried to her side. "What's up?" I asked.

"The village wants Mama's house to build a parking lot," she told me in disbelief. The man explained that the Olchick house and property would be taken over by Hastings through

86

eminent domain which meant that the government, had the right to appropriate private property for public use. In this case the house was to be demolished for local business parking. "Get out of here!" Anna screamed at the man, waving her hands in the air as my mother translated his explanation. He left in a hurry but that was not the end of the matter.

Before the end of the week, other officials came over to survey and measure. Every room in the house was photographed and noted: "Old floors out of level....No lights.... Wall leaning out of plumb by at least seven inches.... Deteriorated plaster walls...Settling of building indicated." The next few months our family's life was turned upside down as my mother hired a lawyer to try and save the old house but we didn't stand a chance. Halfheartedly, we hunted for another place to live though Anna refused to come with us to look at any. "I will stay here until I die," she stated more than once throughout the ordeal.

Thirty years is a long time in one place. Anna loved every inch of that house and property: the cozy kitchen where she cooked countless meals on her big black stove, the upstairs bedroom with its low-ceiling that seemed to embrace her and Vincenty as they slept, the grapevines and roses and a vegetable patch rich with organic soil. How could she give up the American dream she had worked so hard to achieve? It wasn't easy. She and Vincenty were in their seventies, too old to pick up and move on, but when the village turned off their water, Anna finally realized the dream was over and sadly began packing.

On July 10, 1956, Anna and Vincenty Olchick closed the door to their home for the last time. Arm in arm, they walked stoically through the front gate with the morning glories in full bloom, down their gravel lane and never looked back. In an ironic twist of fate, it was exactly thirty years to the day- July 10, 1926, that they had first stepped foot into the house on 4 Spring Street.

CHAPTER THIRTEEN

The two of them slowly turned down Dock Street carrying a few of their possessions. They trudged along the railroad tracks heading south towards the familiar tenement buildings they once lived in and climbed up a short incline to a rear apartment where they rested awhile, watching trains wiz by and smoke billowing above the saw-toothed roofs of the Anaconda Wire and Cable Company. "We've come a long way, and we're right back where we started, eh, Vincenty," said Anna before entering the new place they chose to live out their remaining years. Vincenty, looked around the small rooms, saw a light switch on the wall and flicked it on. "Well Anichka, you have electricity for the first time. Now, go and make me a soup for supper," he said taking out his pipe and tobacco.

I marveled at my grandparents' capacity to endure their removal from the home they both cared for so much. They seemed to settle into their new quiet life together, refusing to live with either my parents who had moved to nearby Dobbs Ferry, or with Antoinette's family in Yonkers. Vincenty spent time fishing on the Hudson River and Anna learned to cook on a gas stove, had a little garden in back and tended her indoor potted plants. They loved Hastings, would never consider leaving their adopted village and we visited them frequently, bringing groceries, sitting with them, chatting. On one of those visits, my mother noticed a far away look in Anna's eye: she talked with difficulty, her speech was slurred. Sophie brought her to a doctor immediately. Anna had suffered a stroke and was hospitalized for the first time in her life.

Anna never fully recovered; she needed nursing home care which she resisted but had to accept. We brought flowers to her room, old fashioned pink and red roses in summer, frilly-blossomed marigolds in fall, lilies of the valley and violets in springtime. Vincenty sat silent by her bedside- they had no need to talk, what was there to say? They had been through life together and now that they lived apart they accepted what fate handed them. My grandfather never missed a visit to his wife of over fifty years, and it was

Vincenty and Anna Olchick say goodbye to each other on the grounds of a Westchester County nursing home on a wintry day in 1968.
Photo by Carol Marie Davis

on his last visit while holding her hand as he had when they first met, that Anna slipped away.

My grandmother looked peaceful. A faint smile on her lips turned up at the corners, her hands were folded in prayer. She wore a plain print dress and a bright red shawl across her shoulders. By her side we placed a sprig of roses, a small loaf of bread and a packet of salt. She was buried on a windy day in March 1968, next to her sons who had passed away before her. She was eighty-two.

Anna bequeathed little of monetary value: a golden wedding ring, a cut glass sugar bowl, a few dollars to cover the expenses of nursing care for herself and Vincenty. Her legacy lives on though, in those she left behind; children, grandchildren, great grandchildren, and great, great grandchildren; a family who remembers the way she lived, the things she did. She had an amazing capacity to persevere; to survive the daily rigors of hard work while remaining essentially who she was- a strong, opinionated woman who was unafraid to live life to the fullest. Earthy, stubborn, and harsh at times, she had the heart of a peasant, always keeping the needs of her family first and foremost in mind.

EPILOGUE

When Anna died, Vincenty shuttled back and forth living with my parents and Antoinette's family until he, too, needed nursing care. At the age of ninety-two, he passed away and joined his beloved Anna and their three sons.

I sometimes visit the place where I grew up in Hastings and I hardly recognize the village, it has changed so. I walk to where my grandparent's home once stood and gaze about the bustling parking lot named Steinschneider Plaza after a 1930s village mayor. I go to the spot where Anna once had a garden and picture her bent over the rows of cabbages and mint, telling the little seedlings to grow strong and be fruitful and I smile. "I will never forget you," I tell Anna in my heart as I turn away and watch the sun dip beyond the palisades along the river.

ANNA'S
FAVORITE
RECIPES

Brown Bread

Preparing and cooking food was deeply rooted in my grandmother's soul, but the means by which she cooked is sometimes difficult to replicate. She used oral recipes passed down through generations of ancestors, using a pinch of this and a handful of that. Be this as it may, I have selected a few favorites adding my own, up-to-date measurements to recall the tastes and smells of her kitchen.

Blini

Scald 2 cups of milk and when it's cool, stir in one package of yeast (Anna used a cake of fresh yeast, but dry active yeast is okay), one tablespoon of sugar, and one and a half cups of flour in a ceramic bowl. Cover it with a towel and let rise in a warm place for one hour.

In another bowl, beat 3 egg yolks with 1 tablespoon of salt, 1 tablespoon of melted butter, and 1/2 cup of flour and add to the risen batter. Set aside. Meanwhile, separately, beat 3 egg whites until stiff and fold into the batter.

Heat skillet with 2-3 tablespoons of butter and spoon in the batter in 3-4 inch circles and fry. When bubbles appear, flip over but don't burn, they should be light golden brown in color. Serve hot with melted butter and honey. (Tip- to keep the cooked blini warm while frying others, put them on a plate in a 200 degree F oven).

Blini

Easter Pasca Bread

INGREDIENTS

1 package of dry yeast or 1 cake of fresh yeast
1 cup scalded milk
¼ cup of lukewarm water
½ cup of sugar
2 teaspoons of salt
½ cup of softened butter
5 cups of sifted flour
2 eggs
¼ cup of golden raisins
1 egg white

Soften yeast in warm water and set aside. Combine scalded milk, sugar, salt and butter and cool until lukewarm. Stir in 2 cups of flour and eggs and mix well, then stir in softened yeast; add raisins and remaining flour to make a soft dough. Let rest for 10 minutes and then knead for 10 minutes on a lightly floured board until the dough is smooth and elastic. Place in a buttered bowl, turning the dough all around so that the entire surface is well greased. Cover with a cloth and let rise in a warm place until doubled in bulk.

Easter Pasca Bread

Punch the dough down and let rise again for one hour or more. Then divide the dough into 2 balls, cover and let rise another 10 minutes. Divide each ball of dough into 3 parts and roll each part into a long snake about 18 inches long. Then braid the 3 pieces together. Put in buttered loaf pan, cover, and let rise 1 hour. Brush with 1 beaten egg white and bake in moderate oven at 350 degrees F for about 30 minutes or until done.

Garlicky Chicken Soup

INGREDIENTS

    1 (3 pound) whole chicken with giblets
    10 cloves garlic
    1 onion
    4 stalks celery, quartered
    4 parsnips, quartered
    4 carrots, quartered
    bunch of parsley, cut
    salt and pepper to taste,
    1 sprig of thyme
    water to cover

Cut chicken in pieces and put it and the giblets in a large soup pot with water, garlic, onions, celery, parsnips, carrots, thyme, and half of the parsley (save the other half to cut up for a garnish). Heat and simmer until the chicken falls off the bones about 2 hours.

Remove the bones, giblets and skin; skim off fat; season with salt and pepper; sprinkle with the rest of fresh parsley and serve with good brown bread.

garlicky Chicken Soup

Brown Bread

This is a time consuming recipe the way my grandmother made it. First you must use a leaven which is mixed in a bowl and left in a warm place (in back of the stove) at 75 degrees F for two days. The leaven includes 2 cups of wholegrain rye flour, 7/8 cup warm water and a sourdough rye starter saved from your last batch of bread. If you don't have the starter, you can make it from 9 tablespoons of whole ground rye flour, ¼ cup of warm water and a pinch of caraway seeds.

To make the dough, dissolve ¼ cup of dark molasses in 1 cup of hot water and add 1 cake of fresh yeast. Then add 1 ¼ dry rye bread crumbs and mix together. Let stand for 30 minutes. Add the leaven, then 2 cups of whole meal rye flour and 1 ¾ cups of whole meal wheat flour and 2 teaspoons of salt. Mix to form dough, then turn it on a wooden floured surface and knead for 10 minutes.

Let dough rise in a covered bowl in warm place for 2 hours until doubled in size. Place on the lightly floured wooden board, punch down and make a round loaf. Let it rise again on a greased baking tin covered with a towel for 45 minutes. Meanwhile heat oven to 450 degrees F.

Slash the bread with cross on top and bake for 15 minutes. Reduce the oven temperature to 400 degrees F and bake for 35 minutes more. The bread is done when it sounds hollow when you tap it on the bottom. Cool; slice a nice chunk and serve with butter.

Brown Bread

Mushroom Kasha

Mix 1 cup of kasha (buckwheat groats) with 1 egg and 1/3 cup of sliced sautéed mushrooms- my grandfather picked wild mushrooms for this recipe, but you can use your favorite grocery store variety. Stir fry this mixture in 2 tablespoons of butter until the egg is cooked and buckwheat is separated.

Add 2 cups of boiling chicken stock (make sure to save some from the Garlicky Chicken Soup recipe), salt and pepper and simmer covered, for 10 minutes. Fluff with fork before serving warm.

Mushroom Kasha

Potato and Cheese Pierogi
Potato/cheese Filling

11/2 pounds of potatoes
2 tablespoons butter
4 tablespoons milk
½ pound of Farmers's cheese
salt and pepper to taste

Potato and Cheese Pierogi

Boil peeled potatoes, drain and mash with butter and milk. Add cheese and season with salt and pepper. Set aside to cool.

Meanwhile, in a large bowl, mix 2 cups of sour cream, 4 ½ cups of flour, 2 eggs, 2 teaspoons of salt and 2 tablespoons of vegetable oil. Knead into a soft, pliable dough; cut in half and let rest, covered, for 10 minutes.

Roll out each half into a thin circle. Using a drinking glass, cut the dough into round circles and fill them, 1 tablespoon at a time in the center of each circle with the above potato-cheese filling. Fold over to form a half-moon shape and press edges together with fingers. Be sure the edges are sealed well to prevent the filling from running out.

Cook in boiling salted water for about 8-10 minutes, stirring gently with a wooden spoon to separate them. Pierogies will be ready when you see them puff up. Drain and place on a dish. Serve warm with melted butter or sautéed sliced onions.

Cabbage Soup

INGREDIENTS

2-3 pounds of cabbage sliced into ½-inch strips

2 tablespoons vegetable oil

3 tablespoons minced garlic

1 cup of chopped carrots

1 28-ounce can pureed tomatoes

1 small can of tomato paste

½ cup of brown sugar

¼ cup of lemon juice

pinch of salt & black pepper

1 bay leaf

Heat oil and sauté garlic in a large soup pot over medium fire until garlic is soft, about 2 minutes. Add onion and sauté until soft as well. Add 3 cups of water, carrots, tomatoes, tomato paste, brown sugar, bay leaf and simmer for 10 minutes until carrots are tender, about 10 minutes. Take out the bay leaf and discard.

Mash the above mixture in a bowl until it is a coarsely blended. Return the sauce mixture to the pot, add lemon juice, cabbage strips, and 3 cups of water. Simmer until cabbage is cooked about 2 hours. Add more water to desired consistency. Add salt and pepper to taste and serve with a topping of sour cream.

Bread Pudding

INGREDIENTS

3-4 cups of stale bread cubes

3 eggs

1 quart of milk

1/3 cup honey

1 teaspoon vanilla

¼ teaspoon salt

¾ cup of raisins

¼ teaspoon cinnamon

Butter a 2 quart baking dish and spread bread cubes on the bottom. In a large bowl, beat eggs until nice and foamy; add milk, honey, vanilla and salt.. Blend well and pour over bread cubes, letting the bread soak throughly. Sprinkle raisins and cinnamon over top and bake in a preheated oven at 350 degrees F for about 1 hour or until a knife inserted in the mid comes out clean. Serve hot with cream.

Bread Pudding

ACKNOWLEDGEMENTS

To go back in time takes the help of many people. I am grateful to those who have contributed to my knowledge of both family memories and historical facts. My sister Priscilla Cant, and cousins Sylvia Schezzini and Rosita Winkler shared their memories of the past freely and I thank them from the bottom of my heart. Special thanks to Muriel Olssson, Fatima Mahdi, Margaret Crawford, Susan Maggiotto, and Dr. Stephen Paczolt for providing old maps, deeds, and photographs; to Anna Graves for patiently translating old family letters from Russian to English, and to the Hastings Historical Society for publishing my first memoir *They Paved Paradise and Put up a Parking Lot*. My deep appreciation goes to my children Rachel Anne Jagareski, Russell Thane Aveney, and Amanda Lael Davis for their love and encouragement, and to my life-time companion Dr. Alex Roth for his unending support. I am indebted beyond words to my mother Sophie Olchick Venuto who loved us all and to my grandmother Anna Anisovich Olchick who made everything possible.

This story is based in part out of my curiosity for the early history of my remarkable grandmother who spoke so little of the hard life she had in Belarus, formerly Byelorussia. Although I embroidered the first years of her life, the facts and texture are drawn from folklore and research material provided by the Library of Congress, Washington, D.C., The Statue of Liberty-Ellis Island Foundation, Hastings Historical Society, Hastings-on-Hudson, New York, and from my favorite antiquarian bookstore- Rachel and Dan's Old Saratoga Books in Schuylerville, New York.

9 781936 343836